THE PRIESTESS AND PEARLS

Rituals for the Journey to the Divine Feminine

Georgia van Raalte

BLACK MOON PUBLISHING
CINCINNATI, OHIO
USA

Black Moon Manifesto

It is the Will and mission of Bate Cabal/Black Moon to effectively manifest unique and insightful occult Works for the esoteric community in a manner that is unfettered by commercial considerations.

BlackMoonPublishing.com

blackmoonpublishing@gmail.com

Design and layout by
Jo Bounds of Black Moon

With heartfelt thanks to Dave Moore (*Pathworking for Liber Lazuli and Persephone's Mass*), Marco Visconti (*The Rite of the White Spring and Liber Sophia*), and Theodore Elser (*Liber Sophia and The Equinox of the Bees*), for offering to me their knowledge, wisdom, guidance and fire as I undertook this work.

ISBN: 978-1-890399-78-8

United States • United Kingdom • Europe • Australia • India • Japan

CONTENTS

Introduction 7

A Pathworking for Liber Lazuli 9

The Rite of the White Spring 16

    Words from the White Spring 21

Persephone's Mass 23

    I. The Actors 23

    II. The Preparation of the Temple 23

    III. The Rite 25

Liber Sophia 46

    Introduction 46

    Intimation 51

    I. Of the Furnishings of the Temple 53

    II. Of the Officers of the Mass 54

    III. Of the Ceremony of the Introit 54

    IV. Of the Ceremony of the Opening of the Veil 58

    V. Of the Office of the Collects 61

    VI. Of the Consecration of the Elements (Pentecost) 64

    VII. Of the Office of the Anthem 66

    VIII. Of the Consummation of the Elements

        (Fear and Trembling) 68

The Equinox of the Bees 70

    Introduction 70

Preparing the Body 71

Preparing the Altar 72

Moving into Stillness 73

Performing the Rite 74

I. The Blessing of the Bee 75

II.Gloria Mundi 76

III. Exploration of the Inside 77

IV. Composition of the Garden Temple 79

V. Invocation of Our Lady Rising 80

VI. The Sacrifice 82

VII. Contemplation 83

The Feast 84

Epilogue 85

Introduction

A year after finishing the last of these rituals, I find myself sitting here attempting to write an introduction to this book. It is a surprisingly difficult task; in fact, I have been struggling with it weeks. It is difficult to speak about the inception and creation of these rituals. They were written with friends who are no longer friends. They catalysed transformation through fights and strife as much as they did through love and understanding. To tell the stories of these rituals would be to confess some of my most intimate experiences. To speak of their results, too, would be to confess my complexes, my misunderstandings, and all my heartbreak. These ghosts chase my fingers as I try to type these words; yet, what is publishing but a form of exorcism? I cast my thoughts, memories, dreams, creations out into the world. In the eyes of the reader whom I cannot see, they become something else entirely. My thing becomes no thing becomes new thing.

These rituals trace the waves and curves of my path to the divine. It is my hope that they may act as illumination, or as a map for your own journey. The creation of these rituals were processes of gaining knowledge; their performance brought understanding. Writing these rituals was an exercise in creative devotion. Performing them was a lesson in the reality of magic, and the irresistibility of its circuits and waves.

Rituals are generally seen as having an aim, a point. I'm not sure that any of these rituals do. These rituals are experiments in reality and relationality. My intentions with these works were more like hypotheses; each ritual proved a hypothesis wrong, and thus brought

me closer to the truth. They are meditations and mystery plays. Aimless games that teach the divinity of flesh, and the fleshiness of the divine. They seek only to open the user to experience; to take them to the contact point. They are offerings, ritual dances that teach and invoke, great outpourings of energy, emotion, time, passion, all an offering of All to Her. They are living altars, mandalas. A maze.

These rituals utilise juxtaposition and movement across boundaries. They are sites of liminality, and thus power. They are games, toys; and the most serious technology we have ever had. These rituals offer a space of communitas, a suspended community in the liminal, ritual space, a mode of being with others that is utterly transformative.

These rituals are magpie nests, built from all the shiny symbolism and structure I could lay my greedy hands upon. These rituals can be anything you want them to be; solemn rites or fantasies, mystery plays or literary provocations. Their reading offers a carnival of images in which to saturate your soul. Their performance offers lessons in being, in doing, and in communitas. You may gain as much or as little from them as from a journey on the train. Abide for a while, and watch the phantasmic flora and fauna glide past the window of your literary vision. You will not seem to move; yet it will be that you have travelled very far.

A Pathworking for Liber Lazuli

You are in a clearing in a wooded area. To the south is a fire burning in a fire pit. To the west is a brook, flowing over rocks. To the east, the land drops off sharply, and you gaze out at clouds floating in the distance and birds flying through the blue sky. To the north, the land rises up steeply, and there is the mouth of a cave.

In the center of the clearing before you rises a low stone altar, roughly shaped. On the altar are a simple pottery cup and stone knife, hewn of pale flint. There are wax spots on the altar, where old candles have burned down. There is also a pentacle of bronze, and a porcelain incense burner, within which burns resin on coals.

Behind you, the fire in the fire pit burns high: you can hear the wood crackle, and smell the pungent smoke. The stream continues to play and gurgle in the West, and the gentle cry of birds comes from the east. It is always quiet to the north.

Tipping your head to the altar, you walk towards the mouth of the cave. Though the entrance appears small, you find you can enter without ducking your head. The light is dim inside, and has no clear source; it seems as though the phosphorescent glow comes from the stones of the cave itself. As your eyes accustom to the dim light, you see three passages ahead of you. From the passage to the right comes a single beam of moonlight, which has stolen through a crack in the cave wall. On the left, the smoke from a sacrificial fire. The path in front of you is blocked by a shifting figure; as you step forward she solidifies, dressed only in stars and the snake. With a smile, she pulls aside the heavy leather curtain that lay over the entrance to the path;

silver light beams across the dull cave walls. Offering the guardian a nod of recognition, you pass through the curtain and begin to tread the path ahead.

The rock is hard and uneven under your feet, the rough walls of grey stone arch above you. There is enough space below the ceiling for you to walk with your head high. The walls of the cave are dark, the silver light shining as a beacon up ahead. As you walk towards the light the walls appear to fall away; the passage widens and you realise you are no longer walking through rock, but tread a thin path between great trees and dense underbrush. You continue down the forest path until the canopy opens up ahead of you, and you find yourself standing at the edge of a large, grassy field, bordered by thick swathes of nodding wheat. There are many figures here, dancing in a complex circular pattern: there are deer, and other wild things, fauns and dryads and elves, all dancing. Their laughter ripples across the meadow; the sun shines bright and the air is cool and clear. The breeze winds through the old oaks on the edge of the clearing, making them sing.

The dancers, ecstatic with the song of the trees, grow frenzied; their circle revolves ever quicker, in ever more complex patterns. You begin to walk around the edge of the dancing circle, but are quickly pulled into its center. Amidst the whirling tails and limbs there is a moment of space and you see her once more, the star-skirted guardian, dancing a silent duet with her lover the sun. The circle revolves once more and the vision of the goddess disappears; your arms are grasped by hand and tentacle and claw, and you are spun in ecstatic whirlwind circles, round and round until you emerge on far side of the circle; on the other side of the mass of bodies you see the passage by which you had come to this place; the entrance now appears a crawl-space. Turning from the old stone and the whirling dancers and the happy infinity of the field, you face the

path ahead of you.

The path leads back into the forest: down a crumbling, rocky slope to a crack in a sheer rock wall. The crack fits your shape perfectly, and you enter the dark stone cave. The tunnel is flat here, and the path marked with white stones. Ahead of you is an archway, tall and wide, and hung across with heavy drapes. Painted on the curtain is a silver moon, waning, and nine purple cups, overflowing into one another. From beyond the curtain comes a breath and a smile, a movement of the air. You pull the heavy cloth aside, and enter.

You find yourself in a vast, echoing chasm. So vast, in fact, you cannot see the ceiling as it arcs towards the heaven; there appear to be stars, nestled amongst the rock; perhaps they are chinks from the light outside.

Ahead of you lies a vast, inky lake, its waters veiled by violet mists. The light, the dim glow of these cracked stars, filtered purple through the clouds. There is thick smoke, too, purple and blue; the smoke comes from the center of the lake, where a censer burns upon an altar.

Across the water, between the mists, you hear the thin note of some ancient flute: as your eyes grow accustomed to the half-light, you notice there are figures, dancing, on the edge of the lake; among the mists, it seems as though they are dancing across the water.

You see something shining amongst the smoke and gloom at the far side of the lake; your eyes meet other eyes, dark, shining eyes. Hecate sits, veiled and waiting, at the back of the cave, past the well of the moon-pool. The strange thin music of the lute cannot disguise her gentle sobbing.

You walk forward, into the dark water; feel the cool tides lap against your bare legs. You continue; the water, though cool, is refreshing, and doesn't reach past your knees. You wade out into the center of the lake, where the altar lies with its smoking censer.

As you draw close, you see that the altar is not made of the same dark rock as the walls of the cavern; the altar is made of a single, perfect piece of amethyst, sparkling clear and hewn with nine sides. Surrounding the altar, suspended in the dark water, are overflowing sprays of violets and roses, of lilies and hyacinths, all white and purple. On the altar itself, a single narcissus and a pomegranate, split in two, with the red seeds tumbling across the amethyst altar, staining the soft petals of the narcissus.

As you stand there enraptured at the altar, the strange music of the lute is joined by a song:

My God, how I love Thee!
With the vehement appetite of a beast I hunt Thee through the
    Universe.
Thou art standing as it were upon a pinnacle at the edge of some
    fortified city. I am a white bird, and perch upon Thee.
Thou art My Lover: I see Thee as a nymph with her white limbs
    stretched by the spring.
She lies upon the moss; there is none other but she:
Art Thou not Pan?
I am He. Speak not, O my God! Let the work be accomplished
    in silence.
Let my cry of pain be crystallized into a little white fawn to run
    away into the forest!
Thou art a centaur, O my God, from the violet-blossoms that
    crown Thee to the hoofs of the horse.
Thou art harder than tempered steel; there is no diamond beside
    Thee.
Did I not yield this body and soul?
I woo thee with a dagger drawn across my throat.
Let the spout of blood quench Thy blood-thirst, O my God!

Thou art a little white rabbit in the burrow Night.
I am greater than the fox and the hole.
Give me Thy kisses, O Lord God!
The lightning came and licked up the little flock of sheep.
There is a tongue and a flame; I see that trident walking over the sea.
A phœnix hath it for its head; below are two prongs. They spear the wicked.
I will spear Thee, O Thou little grey god, unless Thou beware!
From the grey to the gold; from the gold to that which is beyond the gold of Ophir.
My God! but I love Thee!
Why hast Thou whispered so ambiguous things? Wast Thou afraid, O goat-hoofed One, O horned One, O pillar of lightning?
From the lightning fall pearls; from the pearls black specks of nothing.
I based all on one, one on naught.
Afloat in the æther, O my God, my God!
O Thou great hooded sun of glory, cut off these eyelids!
Nature shall die out; she hideth me, closing mine eyelids with fear, she hideth me from My destruction, O Thou open eye.
O ever-weeping One!
Not Isis my mother, nor Osiris my self; but the incestuous Horus given over to Typhon, so may I be!
There thought; and thought is evil.
Pan! Pan! Io Pan! it is enough.
Fall not into death, O my soul! Think that death is the bed into which you are falling!
O how I love Thee, O my God! Especially is there a vehement parallel light from infinity, vilely diffracted in the haze of this

mind.

I love Thee.

I love Thee.

I love Thee.

Thou art a beautiful thing whiter than a woman in the column of this vibration.

I shoot up vertically like an arrow, and become that Above.

But it is death, and the flame of the pyre.

Ascend in the flame of the pyre, O my soul! Thy God is like the cold emptiness of the utmost heaven, into which thou radiatest thy little light.

When Thou shall know me, O empty God, my flame shall utterly expire in Thy great N. O. X.

What shalt Thou be, my God, when I have ceased to love Thee?

A worm, a nothing, a niddering knave!

But Oh! I love Thee.

I have thrown a million flowers from the basket of the Beyond at Thy feet, I have anointed Thee and Thy Staff with oil and blood and kisses.

I have kindled Thy marble into life—ay! into death.

I have been smitten with the reek of Thy mouth, that drinketh never wine but life.

How the dew of the Universe whitens the lips!

Ah! trickling flow of the stars of the mother Supernal, begone!

I Am She that should come, the Virgin of all men.

I am a boy before Thee, O Thou satyr God.

Thou wilt inflict the punishment of pleasure—Now! Now! Now!

Io Pan! Io Pan! I love Thee. I love Thee.

O my God, spare me!

Now!

It is done! Death.

Stirring from your awed contemplation of the mysteries, your eyes fail to find those of the singer across the water; her song complete, she has withdrawn, once more, to her sanctum. Uttering a prayer of ecstasy, you turn, leaving the cavern by the same path across the water you had tread before. Entering the cave passage once more, you see a rough etching on the stone wall; it is the goddess in dancing once more, bathed in a rainfall of bay leaves. Looking at the path ahead of you, you find there is no slope to return; the stone path lies straight before you.

You tread the passage carefully but still are almost tripped by a sharp step up; catching yourself, you know you will soon be home. You continue to walk; suddenly, the walls open up around you, and you find yourself back in that first clearing from which you had started, with the simple, stone altar in front of you. You trace the clearings' circle clockwise, and return to kneel before the altar, and the Northern paths. Gathering your disparate shreds about you, you open your eyes.

The Rite of the White Spring

Song

Omari tessala marax,
tessala dodi phornepax.
amri radara poliax
armana piliu.
amri radara piliu son';
mari narya barbiton
madara anaphax sarpedon
andala hriliu.[1]

Invocation

Prologema:

IO! —
I dreamt of a vast field of rye,

---

1 This song is the song of BABALON, and evokes Her presence during this rite. It was first recorded by Aleister Crowley in ARN, the Cry of the 2nd Aethyr. Its translation is as follows:
    I am the harlot that shaketh Death.
    This shaking giveth the Peace of Satiate Lust.
    Immortality jetteth from my skull,
    And music from my vulva.
    Immortality jetteth from my vulva also,
    For my Whoredom is a sweet scent like a seven-stringed
        instrument,
    Played unto God the Invisible, the all-ruler,
    That goeth along giving the shrill scream of orgasm

And mountains in the distance
A broken, bronzed and shattered sky,
And a blue plane of existence
On the breeze, faint screams
And the smell of burning
For my Lord has given me dreams
Of broken bones and yearning
Of trees in ink, and ink on skin;
Of pomegranates, and new Sin.
Burn, become light and heat and help.
Melt.

Verse:

Oh, infinite stars
Stars reflected on dark water
Water made red by her blood,
Blood she bleeds for him,
For he is jealous,
With a jealousy grown from fear
He fears for she can bleed eternal
Her bleeding knows not lack or loss;
Her loss of blood is all resurgence,
A resurgence breaking floodgates,
For a flood of blood is hers,
She bleeds eternal,
And knows the life which rises from red springs.

Chorus:

Oh, Rhiannon,
My Lady Aloft,

Come to me
Three-in-one,
One-in-three

Oh, Arawn,
My Lord Hunting,
Follow me,
Three-in-one,
One-in-three.

Verse:

As the spirits dance faster,
The images become bright:
Cain and his puppet-master,
Simeon and his light:
Babalon and her Beast.

My Lord and Lady
Dance around the springs
They are all whiring,
Gleaming, dancing things,
For they know neither night nor day
The gods know only eternal play;
They know the mother's flowing
Is the mirror of the hermit
They know the pomegranate's glowing
They know the play where the spermat—
Oza and the egg meet, thus:
Mount not,
Control not,
Be ridden,

Let them in.
Oh, dark and stormy spirit,
made of chalk and stars and prayers;
Oh, spirit of refracting light,
filled with blood that does not flow
Oh, my lords and ladies fair;
Smother us who seek to know

Oh Lady of the Springs,
Lord of the Clay,
Oh Lady of the night time
And Lord of the day
We seek to hear your silence,
We seek to feel your absent touch.

Chorus:

Oh, Rhiannon,
My Lady Aloft,
Come to me
Three-in-one,
One-in-three

Oh, Arawn,
My Lord Hunting,
Follow me,
Three-in-one,
One-in-three.

Verse:

For we have witnessed great charges,
Clashes,

All the machines of war.
And thus we visit scenes we've lived before.
And so, My Lord, my Lady;
do with us what Spring does with the cherry trees;
Wrap us in light and pain.
Swallow us, dissolve us, excrete us;
Cry blood tears salty with the taste of our stain.

The cunt of the mother
the breasts of the lover.
The sweat, and the blood,
which is death and godhood.
Dance beyond the bordered glade
Hide within the dappled shade
 Know anthills, wormholes, foxes dens
Know false gods frolic in woodland fens
Know this, and nothing more:
We are divine, we kneel in awe

Io pan, my love,
Convince them of my truth
There is naught below, and naught above;
There is no faith, there is no proof.

The farce of human time
The sinking in the brine
Of ancient tides.
Care not; think not on the end.
Grasp not; seek not to tame or bend.
 I have no shame, nor fear;
For my gods are already here.

Chorus:

Oh, Rhiannon,
My Lady Aloft,
All for me:
My Three-in-one,
My One-in-three.
Oh, Arawn,
My Lord Hunting,
All for me,
My Three-in-one,
My One-in-three.

Words from the White Spring

(scrawled on a scrap of paper after the event)

Infected with the cosmic giggle, I roam among the springs, meet goblins and groupies among the flashing lights — know them, laughing amongst the stream falling from the ceiling. The onlookers look on, as if I am one possessed for that is precisely what I am — all filled with that giggle and orgasm which doesn't befit writing, those dark things which make me wriggle, wriggle in the deep under the thin water streaming from the ceiling.

Jump in — meet your limits fool, have the breath knocked from your lungs and the cold toes and the numb legs and oh! he is here he was always here he was here before your begging and now he is gone all gone but you are not empty not empty no, but aware of every space and line for what was filled with water is now filled with wine.

For they came they came they filled and they danced and they

said the secret things no one knows and they said it to me and only me and no one else and they let me hear it only me, only me they let me hear that cosmic giggle which drives men mad — but not so me for I danced with the gods you didn't know existed and their lights caught my tail feather and burned and burned and burned and the whole bird went alight — and burned for a moment bright and bright and burning burning until he is quenched, quenched for the joy of love and learning.

Learning ha! My lord learns not, teaches not — only fills, fills up until you're full and pouring out and overflowing waterfalls from mouth and eyes and arms and ears until you're empty empty empty and yet laughter spills from every orifice the laughing fills what is empty and I am completed in your laughing.

Be careful, though — these are dark gods we play with, and their coming is not what you think — discord, the discord that makes the song sweet. They bid me make a mess, and be all passion, and to drive out thought — to drive out will, and act only through instinct, the instinct of a child and beast.

Persephone's Mass

I. The Actors

- Two Novices
- Squire
- Celebrant
- Herald
- Everyman
- Babalon

II. The Preparation of the Temple

Lights low, curtains closed and hung with silks. Furniture removed, floor scattered with cushions. Back Altar decked with Fresh Fruit and Flowers; upon it lies a jug of wine thickened with Myrrh and Spices. Side Altar covered with Silk, decked with Flowers and Fruits. Altar in the Window is heavy with Offerings. It is surrounded with Plants, covered in Silk and lain with Pomegranates, Dates, Red Fruits and Fine Spices; with Lilies, Ivy and a Sunflower. Incense of Abramelin burning on the Corner Altar and on the Front Altar three censers: one of Myrrh, one of Frankincense, and one of Dittany of Crete. Upon the Front Altar lie a Marchpane figure of the Holy Family, crafted by the Priestess and placed thereon by Everyman. There is a plate of salt, and cups of Water from the Red Spring, and the White. Beside the Altar are clean towels, dressings and a bowl of water to tend the Holy Wounds. At the center of the

Altar is a space into which the Priestess will be borne aloft. To the left hand of this space lies a simple Cup; to the right, a Paten of Cakes of Light, and a Knife.

Upon entering the Temple, congregants will be asked to divest themselves of coats, bags and shoes. They must take their Offering and place it upon the altar. They are then offered the hospitality of the house: Rose and Mugwort tea, and a single pomegranate seed. Once the congregation has arrived and partaken of the fruit, a thorough Briefing takes place. Once all questions have been answered satisfactorily, and all participation made known, the congregants take their seats along the Pillars of Mercy and Severity. The other actors take their place; the Herald at the Left of the Altar, in Binah, the Squire at the Right, Chokmah. Before the Altar, in Yesod, stands Everyman, emboldened with Sword, Shield and Disk. Behind him, at the back of the room, stand the Celebrant, armed with the Lance. Novice one stands amongst the congregation at Chesed, and Novice two at Geburah. Once arranged thusly the Celebrant retrieves Babalon from her confinement, escorts her to the Altar and places her upon it, in Kether. The Celebrant then retreats, clockwise around Everyman, returning to his place in Malkuth.

With the Participants thus arranged, the Rite becomes a glyph for the crossing of the Abyss. Everyman passes through the ecstasy of Tiphareth, and describes the Path of the Serpent. He traverses in the Emptiness of Knowing in order to gain his Babalon. The Celebrant is placed in Malkuth; this is permissible, for the Celebrant is the Mirror and Double of the Priestess. For Everyman is not true Priest here but the Pharmakos, Scapegoat and Fool. It is the Celebrant who is Adept and Priest. He is the male aspect of Binah, the Peacock, and in this New Rite he takes his place where the whore used to lie. The Rite is thus a play upon the Traditional Mass, one offering a glimpse into the Mystery of the Avalonian Initiation Formula.

III. The Rite

Prologue

Squire:

Come with me, child; walk with me down these dark train tracks, air thick with sweat and grime. Pass through the chain-link fence into Hades' Town.

[The Squire beckons to the Offerings laid on the Altar]

We come bearing gifts, red fruit and rubies. Hold your precious load tight, spill not one drop, for the dogs and vipers surround us. Journey on, past the watching billboard eyes, down the pomegranate-lined avenue.

Consider the mystery of the Seed in the Underground as we approach the rosebud throne and see Her,

[Squire gestures to Babalon]

Supine amongst the ancient roots of that first, broken tree.

The First Hymn

Novice I:

Praise Be the Great Sea
The Deep before the Fall
Our Lady of Salt and Misery

Binah, Mother of All
Praise Be to her Daughter,
BABALON,
The Mother of Slaughter.
For Babalon is lonely,
Our Goddess writhes in mud;
She is flogged and broken,
She is trodden underfoot.
She descends, for us,
To the cave of Inanna
She is anointed with the sacred ochre,
Lain leaking upon the floor.
Our Lady and Mother is reborn;
For every pain and every cruelty,
Every lash, every mortal affront
Only increases the raging strength
Of her Ravaging Cunt,
Passive and lifeless as a clam shell
Swallowing feces and spitting out pearls.
For our Lady has no use for Vitriol
Our Whore has no hard crystal shell
She knows the refraction of stars in space
Her starry skin is all out-pouring
Her cuts bleed afresh every time.
But this is her spell,
Her overflowing
For pain and joy walk hand in hand:
And this is what the Whore knows.
She is the abused;
She becomes the abuser.
No safety with this Goddess here.
She is yours in her infinite multiplicity

Novice II:

[*Vengefully*]

Until you cum
For you must end and break her heart
And she is yours no more;

[*Shouting*]

I tell you BABALON will leave you

[*Pause*]

[*Quietly, wistfully*]

She is already gone

[*As to a lover*]

For Our Lady of Abominations is infinite
And you are temporary.
This is the mystery of Nuit,
Languorous in the embrace of her consort;
Temporary and eternal,
The meeting place of all, and naught.
Hers is the mark where force meets form.

[*With feeling*]

Our Lady BABALON is not your vision of debased
    splendour
She is our conflation

The life which is not
The unification of all possibility
With the mundane point.

And one cried to the other and said: [*Loudly!*] Holy, holy, holy,
Lord of Hosts, the whole earth is full of his glory!

The Passage Through the Narrow Gate

Herald:

Standing alone in the middle of a midnight desert, I see the stars
that whirl as a halo around me, and an oasis in the distance. It is
ringed with a wall, and a line of skeletal camels stretches from its
gate. Each monstrous quadruped bows its head to squeeze through
the narrow archway and I know that I must do the same.

But the desert is long, and empty, and though my way lies straight
I can see, from corner of my eye, a host of other temples. There
is the Temple of Thunder, and the Temple of the Lightning Flash;
and a Greater Temple for the pregnant, silent pause between Her
brothers. Shining and spherical, they are of another order than the
desert which I tread.

[*Resigned*]

I must learn the splayed-hoof-walk of the camel among the dunes;
I must learn to trudge among the futile masses if I am to gain the
welcome of that Dark City.

Squire:

So we must journey between star-fortresses;
We must strip, even to our very skin,
That we might fit through the narrow gate.

[*Pause*]
[*Hisses triumphantly*]

At last!
We win the Castle with its endless corridors
marble giving way to rough stone.

[*Softly, as to a lover*]

Round walls, dripping
And the smell of smoke
Proclaim the Holy Caves

Oh, Holy Caves,
Wherein lies the Cup of Abominations,
Supine upon a silken throw
All gleaming jewels and worn-out skin,
Kholled lids and blood-stained chin
Open thighs
Impenetrable eyes

[*Final lines fading away, as if talking of a dream or vision*]

The Second Hymn

Novice II:

Come unto me, my Goddess for I could
Love you ten years before the flood,
And, that you be satisfied,
A thousand years unto your eyes
A decade for each breast, at least,
An aeon for the flesh beneath
A thousand thousand years to go
To every finger, every toe
To skin which is as red as roe
To lips which are as white as snow
The blood removed
Unto my cup
And this I hold aloft to sup

Oh, Innana, Ancient Queen
Of all those things which can't be seen
You are Lady of my dreams
You are She of Silent Screams

Novice I:

You had fallen in the dirt
Your Holy Name had been besmirched
You descended to the cave
So that our darkness You might save
For we are bright

And You are black
And You offer
What we lack
You have delved the depths of filth
Prone as foetus in the piles
Of blood and shit and human guilt
Oh you who know the purple skies
That time has past, you do arise!
All blood and bright bodacious breasts
All matted heart and stinking breath

Oh, Innana,
Our Lady of the Bitter Sea
Give all of it, give every piece,
Give all of it to me!

The Invocation of Stinking Flesh

Everyman:

[*Softly, tenderly; as to a child*]

Oh, my love,
my dark pit
My persecution,
my frothing, writhing fit
You are all.
The epitome of woman
And her greatest shame
You stand tall,

My desire is inhuman
And you are to blame

[*With awe*]

You are life itself,
Splitting boundaries of skin.

[*Rises to his knees, clasps his hands for a moment,
as in prayer; the next lines spoken tenderly, paying
tribute*]

So here you lie,
Supine before the fire,
Fire tracing patterns on your rotting, wrinkled skin;
I will traverse every crevice, every sin
Fingers and eyes tracing
Stretchmarks and scars;
Tongue ears nose
Tracing Black Holes and stars.
Wrinkled leather falling from bones;
Of your skin a coin-purse sewn
For the fisherman —
Yeah I will peel the skin from flesh,
To offer beauty to the blessed.
To hang you all about my throne.

[*Rises onto one bended knee]*
[*Hungrily*]

For you:

My paramour
I will feast forever more
Piece by piece so tender,
Yea I will eat your splendour

[*With desire*]

Oh, my love,
My beautiful, broken whore:
You lie supine for you are paralysed
Your greed by Chaos himself chastised;
For you rode the Great Beast day and night
You fought the good, eternal fight
Until he punctured your intestine,
Split you clean in two:
Strung your insides out upon a vine
Made sweetmeats out of you.
Now you lie,
Twisted and rotting;
Your rose skin turning blue.

[*Everyman rises to his feet*]
[*Says, in submission*]

You are all power,
And I am helpless but to grovel
At the foot of your stinking tower
At your filthy witches' hovel.
To beg you,
Let me pay tribute
To your rotting, rancid wounds
Let my tongue

Trace deep and darkened moons
I am young,
My ancient one with eyes wide
Let me drink the puss that seeps from your side;
Give me my lance!

[*Squire hands Everyman his Lance; Everyman raises it
before Babalon*]

[*With desire; but tenderly*]

My Love
My Whore!
I wish to sup
Your face,
Your buttocks
And your breasts;
I wish to taste your liver,
Your kidneys,
And your lungs.
My love!
I wish to taste the iron on my tongue.
Let me sip
From your bleeding cunt;
Let me drink that sweet, stinking
Wine of immortality.

[*Begging*]

Oh, my Goddess:
Let me escort you to the banquet chamber

Let me offer you my final particle of dust;
Let me thread you onto a smooth cypress pole
Let me smell the warm, spicy scent
Of your roasting flesh
Oh, Goddess, allow me to partake
Of that most forbidden sacrament.

[*Everyman cuts a cross into the center of the sigil on Babalon's chest with the lance; kneels before Her and sups warm blood straight from the cut. After drinking his fill he retreats, kneels with head bowed before her*]

Babalon Speaks

Babalon:

These poor fools.
They worship the red and the pleasure and pain,
The witches and women, and they think that they
    know me?!
Little children play in mud and dare to question the
    truth of the darkest sacrament.
Approach my throne,
Crawl on hands and knees down the Cut glass path.
Fall there, prone,
Pressed against the floor of blood and ash.
Let me trample thee, sister.
For there are no gilded roses here,
No crows nor wheeling gods.
Here, before my rosebud throne,
There is silence, and the slow drip of blood.

You are nothing
Of the worms,
Slithering.
Your wormhood is my joy.

[*Babalon raises her arms aloft*]

I am already here!
I have already said yes!
My legs are already open,
My wide cunt already wet
I do not want you in gold and jewels
For I am sick, and I want filth to match mine.
In dirt is my holy of holies.

I am all your darkness
I am all your lack-of-life
I am all your blood red
I am all your black night
I am every cave and crevice
I am stainèd dawn.

I am Lady of the Abyss;
Lady of the Pomegranate
I am flowing, passive darkness;
I am the midnight flood;
I have no blood
Only thick black ichor
Approach me with your lance

[*Babalon touches Her own bloody chest*]

See me freed

[Babalon licks blood from Her finger]

For I am She who rode the Dragon;
All Abominations spring from me.
I demand you come before me naked,
As a child,
Blood and leaves stuck in your hair,
Eyes open and mind wild
I bid thee bare thy breast, be bold
Fear not my sacral knife
For here dwell Fearful Gods and old
Fear not Their watching eyes.
My secret was always that of the Phoenix
That of the monthly moon
To fall, blackened upon the floor
To rise, red and renewed

[Babalon leaps up, steps forward and wrests Lance from Everyman. Strikes him and pushes him to the floor. Feet dangling over Abyss, head in Yesod. Babalon stands over Everyman, her foot on his stomach, the butt of the Lance on his chest; Kali-esque.]

How to describe my light, my darkness
The pearl I stole and crushed between rotting, pearly teeth.
Broken truths fill thee — the pink bud bursts black
Verily I say to thee rail not against the world of form!
You are the point inside the circle, and thus is all joy.
Now revel, roll in blood,

For ecstasy ends;
Hear tsimtsum, and know that you are temporary.
Oh child, yours is not the path of the meek or the
humble — now is the time of saints: preach to me, my
profit, for dark lights glow in dark waters.

[*Babalon hands Lance to Squire; kneels before
Everyman*]

Kneel with me at the foot of the rood,
Feel the warm red rain soak your skin, your net of hair
Spreadeagled in the sky declare
Thy sacrifice,
For thou art forsaken.
My truth is given to the worm and rose alike,
to the howling wolf and the dying ram.
So worry not for your chariot, my child,
Gild not the edges,
For in the Abyss there is an abundance of Nothing.

[*Babalon rises, and returns to the Altar*]

Only listen to the light, and fear not the Dying God.
Oh, Agori. Thine is the kingdom.
Seek not the Abyss,
For it lies in the pit of thy stomach.

The Mystery of the Eucharist:
Liber Cheth vel Vallum Abiegni

Celebrant:

This is the secret of the Holy Graal, that is the sacred vessel of our Lady the Scarlet Woman, Babalon the Mother of Abominations, the bride of Chaos, that rideth upon our Lord the Beast.

[Babalon picks up her Cup and holds it aloft, then places it back on the Altar.]

Thou shalt drain out thy blood that is thy life into the golden cup of her fornication!

[Everyman steps forward from Yesod to Teth and forward unto Babalon. He presents his chest; Babalon picks up her Knife and cuts a circle gently, as a lover. She places the Knife back on the altar, picks up her Cup and catches the blood in it. Everyman steps back to Teth.]

Thou shalt mingle thy life with the universal life. Thou shalt keep not back one drop.

[Babalon picks up Water from the White Spring on the Altar and pours it into her Cup. She picks up Salt from a plate on the Altar, and sprinkles this into her Cup. She raises the Cup aloft and then places it back on the Altar.]

Then shall thy brain be dumb, and thy heart beat no more, and all thy life shall go from thee; and thou shalt be cast out upon the

midden, and the birds of the air shall feast upon thy flesh, and thy bones shall whiten in the sun.

[*Novice one picks up the silken scarf from off the Altar and blindfolds Everyman, then stands by his side.*]

Then shall the winds gather themselves together, and bear thee up as it were a little heap of dust in a sheet that hath four corners, and they shall give it unto the guardians of the abyss.

[*Novice two forces Everyman to one knee, then remains by his side.*]

And because there is no life therein, the guardians of the abyss shall bid the angels of the winds pass by. And the angels shall lay thy dust in the City of the Pyramids, and the name thereof shall be no more.

[*Pause.*]

Now therefore that thou mayest achieve this ritual of the Holy Graal, do thou divest thyself of all thy goods.

[*Everyman drops the Lance and Sword to the ground.*]

Thou hast wealth; give it unto them that have need thereof, yet no desire toward it.

[*Everyman drops the Disk or Shield to the ground.*]

Thou hast health; slay thyself in the fervour of thine abandonment

unto Our Lady. Let thy flesh hang loose upon thy bones, and thine eyes glare with thy quenchless lust unto the Infinite, with thy passion for the Unknown, for Her that is beyond Knowledge the accursèd one.

Thou hast love; tear thy mother from thine heart, and spit in the face of thy father. Let thy foot trample the belly of thy wife, and let the babe at her breast be the prey of dogs and vultures.

For if thou dost not this with thy will, then shall We do this despite thy will. So that thou attain to the Sacrament of the Graal in the Chapel of Abominations.

[Novices seize him and force him face down upon the floor.]

And behold! if by stealth thou keep unto thyself one thought of thine, then shalt thou be cast out into the abyss forever; and thou shalt be the lonely one, the eater of dung, the afflicted in the Day of Be-with-Us.

[Everyman begins to rise; Novices seize him and force him backwards to the floor. He lies as a Corpse; head resting on Malkuth and feet dangling over the Abyss.]

Yea! verily this is the Truth, this is the Truth, this is the Truth. Unto thee shall be granted joy and health and wealth and wisdom when thou art no longer thou.

Then shall every gain be a new sacrament, and it shall not defile thee; thou shalt revel with the wanton in the marketplace, and the virgins shall fling roses upon thee, and the merchants bend their knees and bring thee gold and spices. Also young boys shall pour wonderful wines for thee, and the singers and the dancers shall sing and dance for thee.

Yet shalt thou not be therein, for thou shalt be forgotten, dust lost in dust.

Nor shall the æon itself avail thee in this; for from the dust shall a white ash be prepared by Hermes the Invisible.

[*Celebrant takes the jug of wine from the corner altar and, standing astride the prone body of Everyman, offers it to Babalon. Babalon picks up her Cup from Altar. He steps forward, kneels before her and adds the wine to Babalon's Cup. He places the jug on her right side. Babalon offers him the Cup and he takes it from her, raising it in awe*]

And this is the wrath of God, that these things should be thus.

[*Celebrant drinks deeply. Offers the Cup to Babalon, who raises it in joy*]

And this is the grace of God, that these things should be thus.

[*Babalon drains the Cup and places it back on the Altar. Celebrant turns to face Malkuth*]

Wherefore I charge you that ye come unto me in the Beginning; for if ye take but one step in this Path, ye must arrive inevitably at the end thereof.

[*Celebrant returns to his place in Malkuth, turning to face Babalon*]

This Path is beyond Life and Death; it is also beyond Love; but that ye know not, for ye know not Love.

And the end thereof is known not even unto Our Lady or to the Beast whereon She rideth; nor unto the Virgin her daughter nor unto

Chaos her lawful Lord; but unto the Crowned Child is it known? It is not known if it be known.

[*Babalon raises her arms*]
[*Pause*]

Therefore unto Hadit and unto Nuit be the glory in the End and the Beginning.

All:

yea, in the End and the Beginning.

The Eucharist

Celebrant:

Omari tessala marax, tessala dodi phornepax.
Amri radara poliax armana piliu.
Amri radara piliu son'; mari narya barbiton
Madara anaphax sarpedon andala hriliu.

[*Chant is maintained as the Herald and Squire, each with their novice, descends to offer Communion to the Congregation.Chanting continues until all have supped.*]

Diogenes' Confession

All Congregants and Actors [barring Babalon upon the Altar and Everyman, who is dead]:
We Confess
The Beauty and Strength of Our Lady Babalon and Her Noble
    Lord Chaos
We Confess

The Sanctity of the Stinking Cup

We Confess
That all of Us, every cell, is Divine

All Adoration
To the Mystery of the Abyss
To She who guards the Gate, and to the Darkness therein.

Closing Hymn

[As the Closing Hymn is sung, Babalon descends from the altar and kneels before the congregation. She removes all Her jewellery, slowly, piece by piece. For She is not in these baubles but in dead skin, and the wanton heart of a child]

Novices:

[Soft, repetitive chanting of Omari tessala marax.]

Herald:

[Kindly, as after much bloodshed]

The rock rolls on, but Sisyphus teaches the truth that empties cities. All is well. We tear down statues, sack temples, raize our relics to the ground. Too few rise from the shitheap and brush the ashes from their robes; too few raise their eyes and see that the sky is still blue, that the heavens did not fall at our insolence. Too few stop to notice as the air rushes in and back out of their lungs. Oedipus, and the cool hand of a girl. All is well.

[Chanting continues until all jewellery removed, whereupon

Babalon climbs atop the prone Everyman, cradled on his chest, and is still]

Epilogue

[*As the squire offers his speech, the Herald offers each of the participants a single pomegranate seed.*]

Squire:

[*Arms raised to the sky*]

Oh Goddess, fill me with falsity, that I may speak these signifiers, that I may circle the infinite light

[*Arms describe a circle as they fall to his sides*]

Before Nuit, there is only the spreading of pentacles. Filled with her bloody light I tell thee there is a further secret, that of the caustic spheres, the meeting cups, rotating bodies; for that which appears a circle is infinite — infinite radiance, infinite change, infinite immutability; and when these circles come together, infinite difference. These secret circles are of a different order than the rod, and this is not an easy path, guarded, as it is, by gargoyles. So let us leave this dark cave now, child. I will bandage your broken skin, plait your hair, matted with blood and glass, into a net of starlight, better to rescue poor fools who tread too far in sleep. Let us leave this rotting rosebud throne — its Queen will remain, hidden, as she is wont to do, playing her games under your skin. Emerging from the cave thou see her not, and rail against the light. Trust thy initiatrix, oh child and fool. Clutch the bandage tight and spill not one drop of that pomegranate blood. Knowing that which is beyond cruelty, measure cruelty with kindness; knowing that which is beyond love, remember we are temporary.

— FIN —

Liber Sophia

00

Introduction

"...Oh, who am I who tower beside this goddess of the twilight air?
The burning doves fly from my heart, and melt within her bosom
there.
I know the sacrifice of old they offered to the mighty queen,
And this adoring love has brought us back the beauty that has
been.
As to her worshippers she came descending from her glowing
skies,
So Aphrodite I have seen with shining eyes look through your
eyes:
One gleam of the ancestral face which lighted up the dawn for me:
One fiery visitation of the love the gods desire in thee!"

— *Aphrodite*, George William AE Russell

"John answered, saying to them all, 'indeed I baptise you with water. However one comes who us mightier than I, the strap of whose sandal I am not worthy to untie. They will baptise you with the Holy Spirit, and fire.'"

— Luke 3.16

ONE

G nosis means direct experience of the divine. It is continuous and it is revolutionary. There is no one messiah, but an infinity of comings. So answer me this: why is there only one Gnostic Mass?

The Gnostic Mass serves two purposes. It is a calling and opening for the common man into the Mysteries; and its Mystery offers a concrete rejuvenation and restoration. With the Gnostic Mass Aleister Crowley sought to create a one-size-fits-all access to the Mysteries. We are not sure it was ever fit for this purpose; it certainly is not today. It is outdated. It still offers rejuvenation (for its Formula is continuous); yet, for every newcomer that it draws into the Mysteries, it alienates another in turn. And none more so than women.

"Now since He is all, and all things are referred to Him, much confusion hath arisen, the Many overwhelming The One. And herein is the reason whereof: and every woman is not a complete image of God in due proportion. Consider these words attentively, and understand what they say not."

— Liber C: Agape vel Azoth

We are searching for something to draw women to the Mysteries; we are no longer convinced that *Liber XV* alone is fit for this goal. For a certain kind of woman, or a woman in a certain place, it will work very well. And we do not dismiss nor denigrate these women, for I myself have been one of them. Yet this exclusivity is a problem, for it can offer women little more than a new and more gilded cage. And worse, for the egregore takes those it alienates and blames them, attributing it to their own repression. It knows nothing of the feminine path and the intimate, intricate god-given trauma of the

masculine gaze.

Thelema is not a naked woman on the altar. It is the sublime ecstasy of the ever-whirring divine duality. It is our approach to this ever-whirring. Our experience of it, our relationship with it, as an individual which is in itself an ever-whirring multiplicity, for the individual is nothing more than a community of stars and cells. The woman on the altar served a purpose; it can still serve one. But it cannot be the end of our work, nor the centre. And this is why Thelema has stagnated since its conception; because it recognised the need for the worship of the goddess, and then found itself unable to enact it; because it feared Her coming.

TWO

Liber XV was designed to offer such a simple illustration of the divine *Formula of ON* that the average Russian peasant could understand it. Unfortunately, I think the average Russian peasant would understand it far better than the average Gnostic Mass-goer today.

This Gnostic Mass operates according to a misconception that abounded in the Victorian world: that the phallus was universal, and without equal counterpart. These monumental Victorians found one path to the gnosis, and enshrined it as the only path. Yet, it is in the nature of gnosis itself that this is a false construction. Imagine a Church where initiation into the clergy came when one wrote and orchestrated a new mass. What a rich, exquisite Church that would be. A Church where, instead of dogma and authority, theology was a living breathing map of the worlds, sewn from the gnosis of the congregation.

In many ways it is of no surprise to me that the O.T.O. has *Liber XV* only as its Mass, and offers training and initiation only

in the phallic path; because its central secret, that of ON, has been operated and understood almost exclusively from the perspective of the phallus – perhaps, can only be operated thus.

"For they understand not that man is the guardian of the Life of God; woman but a temporary expedient; a shrine indeed for the God, but not the God."
                                        —Liber C: Agape vel Azoth

Now, humans like to turn ineffable, incommunicable ideas into metaphor. See the Caduceus: two snakes, wrapped around one another. Picture not the single serpent shooting from the spine, but remember two. Two poles, two snakes, entwined whirring, inside each of us. We call these the masculine and feminine because at this stage in our culture these are the most evocative metaphors we have. Perhaps in time, as our understanding increases, we will be able to surmount this.

Liber XV celebrates the masculine initiation formula, the masculine path to power. It takes the masculine gaze. It celebrates the *Mysteries of ON*—which, though necessarily including masculine and feminine elements, offers subjectivity only to those in the masculine role. Thus we can gender-play the Mass, and this may be a fun and innovative way to viscerally remind the participants of those two snakes; but it is the masculine formula that is enacted nevertheless. *Even gender-played, Liber XV is not sufficient.*

This Formula is a powerful and important one, one which huge swathes of our culture have taken as central. But it is not sufficient, and in trying to make it so, we have mimicked the slave religions, and deeply disadvantaged the growth of of our own. What we need are rituals which celebrate the feminine mysteries, the feminine initiation formulae; we need rituals which celebrate any other

mystery and formula than the singular, specific one used in *Liber XV.*

The Gnostic Mass relies on the Arthurian initiation structure. The Maiden calls forth and rouses the Fool to priesthood; the Priest redeems the woman and places her on the altar, where the primal divinity of the feminine reproductive organs is worshipped symbolically.

This formula cannot simply be switched, for it is an eternal zig-zag, spiralling. This formula assumes that woman is already fallen. Thus I asked myself, what would a mass look like that did not begin by assuming the innate fallenness of humankind?

THREE

I see two women, standing like pillars, and between them a seedling. I see Aphrodite and Psyche; Athena and Ariadne; Hera and the multiplicity of Zeus' consorts. I see Demeter and her daughter Persephone, and the faceless masses marching to the Mysteries. Sophia and Melissa have all these names, and none. Thus the ritual begins with Sophia testing the approaching pythoness, *in memoriam* of these ancient trials which have granted Sophia the sacramental right to consecrate others, for the sake of Her celebration.

Thus Melissa is not a Priestess; the Neophutos is not a Priest. There will be no mention of symbolic virginity in Our Lady's Temple. Melissa was open ere the rite began. With the peach pit, she made her own child. It is a simulacrum of the virgin birth, without that point-less signifier. The Holy Spirit hath impregnated Melissa— we have no need to go poking around to check the integrity of her symbolic hymen.

This is the *Foreshadowing of the Feather*. We are no longer Kundry; we have become Nulla. We are no longer Helen; we have

become Sophia. Yet, this is not the movement of initiation; this is the step to be taken if we are even to begin the story.

For we do not have the new Formula. Not yet. We see the shape, the shadow; but the key has not yet been given.

So what does this immanent ritual do, this *Liber Sophia*, if it does not offer a Formula? It offers a celebration of the mysteries from the feminine perspective; it is that simple, and it is that revolutionary. It is is a celebration. A readdressing of the balance. A ritual that seeks to approach the divine feminine, from the mundane feminine perspective. It offers a path to the mysteries, an avenue of gnosis; an indwelling. It aims to invoke and draw down Sophia by the same movement that it evokes and pulls up Melissa, Priestess before such things were defined by masculine words; emissary of the Honey Bee.

This celebration *doesn't have a magical aim*; it is a mystical act, and as such is unassuaged of purpose. And yet, we do come before the Our Lady with a prayer, a desire, a hope. Like the fertility rituals of old we hope that by enacting Sophia's descent we might provoke a pentecost among us; all the while we recognise that Sophia already indwells among us, and we celebrate this coming with a Mystery play. It is thus that, in this rite, beauty is far more important than accuracy; so too are gnosis and revelation far more important than dogma and formulae.

Intimation

This is not a Mass.

It does not follow the formula of the Dying God, nor does it follow the Formula of Woman-As-Vessel.

There is no Death and Rebirth, for we who are immortal have no need to prove our immortality.

Yet there is a Birth; it is the birth of the Silent Child upon the flower, not the birth of the Whispering Snake.

The word Mass is so defined that there may be no true Mass for Her; since these things are thus, I call this Book not Mass.

This ritual has no Priest or Priestess.
This ritual has no Cup, nor Lance.

This ritual is not an act of Magick.
It is an offering, an act of devotion; it is a communication, a promulgation of the coming of Our Lady.

It does not aim to do anything. It is entirely without intent, unassuaged of purpose.

It is an expression of pure joy; an overcoming of fear.
It is the celebration of Apocalypse.

In Her Name BABALON.

I

Of the Furnishings of the Temple

At the summit of the Temple is an Altar. The Altar is filled all about with fruits[1] and flowers, with offerings and incense; the more plentiful, the better. Offerings may vary according to which aspect of the Godhead favour is sought from; the standard selection can be found in row 3 of *Liber 777*.

The Altar Cloth is of red and gold and white. On the left is a black candle; on the right a white candle. Raised is a candle of deep blue; and in the depths, a candle of red. Behind the Altar is a black pyramid, and at the top thereof is a vesica piscis, and behind the vesica piscis there extends a black cross.

At the foot of the Temple is a womb or cave, with a Veil; the Veil is decorated with a flower or mandala, or some other such vulvic beauty.

Consider the Furnishing of the Temple as an act of devotion and expression of Gnosis in itself. The highest principles are beauty, harmony, attentiveness. The aesthetics of devotion. Precision is less important than beauty; anathema is the 'community centre' draped about with polyester rugs as curtains. The suggestions here are but a vague rubric, and should not be followed slavishly. We have no need for dogmatism or orthodoxy. These things are anathema. We are Gnostics. Our 'creed' is of direct experience and our desire to manifest and communicate this within the mundane. Nothing more.

Revolution has more power than the thousandth repetition.

---

1   Peaches, apples, figs and pomegranates are especially sacred to Our Lady.

II

Of the Officers of the Mass

Melissa and *Sophia* both wear simple, grecian dresses. Melissa wears black or very dark blue; Sophia wears white or cream.

Neophutos should be naked apart from a loincloth. His skin should be covered in ochre or red clay. His hair should be loose, and upon his head two horns. Neophutos may not wear any headdress with a single rising figure, such as the serpent crown. This is anathema to the operation.

A *Master of Ceremonies* should be employed, to see to mundanities of the rite: ushering the Congregants in and out; attending lights and incense; ringing the bell; supplying and removing props; coordinating the Celebration.

III

Of the Ceremony of the Introit

The congregation are admitted. Sophia sits upon the High Altar, looking down from Kether toward Malkuth. Melissa sits in Vajrasana (Thunderbolt pose), head bowed, at Yesod. Neophutos is enwombed in Malkuth.[2]

SOPHIA [*arms raised*]:
Our Lady, who treads upon this Earth

---

2 The Temple is laid out cabbalistically, so as to reflect the Etz Chaim; the Stations of the Rite correspond with the Sephiroth.

Hallowed be thy names.
Thy Queendom has come
Thy Will is done
On Earth, as it is in Heaven
Give us this day our daily wine
And forgive us our stasis
As we forgive those who are trapped in their cages
And lead us into temptation
For we shall deliver ourselves from evil.
In the name of the Mother, the Daughter, and the Fire Qadosh.

Congregants stand.

SOPHIA and all CONGREGANTS: I see Our Lady. Mystery of Mystery She watches and waits, like the waves or a womb. All-eternal, all-powerful, sole creator and nourisher of all that is and will be.

I see Our Lord standing at Her side, Mystery of Mystery, and the fire in His breath is the fire in the mountains.

I see Sophia, emissary of the highest; I see the quickening of Qadosh.

I see Our Mother and Our Father bring forth a Daughter and a Son. I see the veils and the masks that we call Chaos and Babalon.

I see, and my seeing makes me strong. Upon this sight sublime We shall build Our Church.

I see Our Ancestors. They abide among Us.

I see the power of the Living Blood; I see the Miracle of Incarnation.

I see Our Life multitudinous, indistinct and atemporal. We are all that was, and is, and is to come.

This is the Dawning of the Day of Be With Us.

Sophia descends the Tree via the Middle Pillar. She stands before Melissa and offers her a peach. Melissa eats the peach as Sophia speaks.

SOPHIA [*to Melissa*]:
Soft and hollow, how thou dost overcome the hard and full! It dies, it gives itself; to Thee is the fruit!
Be thou the Bride; thou shalt be the Mother hereafter.
To all impressions thus. Let them not overcome thee: yet let them breed within thee.
The least of the impressions, come to its perfection, is Pan.
Receive a thousand lovers; thou shalt bear but One Child.
This Child shall be the heir of the Fate the Father.[3]

Sophia leads Melissa to Tiphareth, where a pot of fertile earth awaits. Melissa plants the peach pit in the pot.

SOPHIA: Come forth into the garden. Here there is darkness but no sleep; silence but no peace; work but no reward.

Sophia leads Melissa to Da'ath; Melissa kneels.

SOPHIA: When thy dust shall strew the earth whereon She walketh, then mayest thou bear the impress of Her foot.

A great bell begins to toll (11). And in the hands of Sophia is a veil so fine and transparent that it is hardly visible. She places this over Melissa, bowing her head reverently. Sophia returns to the Altar, blows out the candles. Darkness.

---

3 *The Book of Lies*, Chapter 4.

SOPHIA: Yea, all is darkness now; and thou art Nulla. Nulla Alogos. No woman, no word, in the garden of nothing.

Oh, my Nulla, She who tends the garden in the Night—see how these invisible flowers grow, darkly gleaming in the darkness. This to be lavished in V.I.T.R.I.O.L.; this to be worshipped with sandalwood.

Sing to the night-time birds, Nulla. For thy Lord will come.

Drumming in the darkness.

Is there any here who can make the speech of No Woman?

Is there any here who would dare to share my place upon this crown, glinting as a Sapphire Star?

Slowly Melissa rises, removing the veil from her face to place it upon her shoulders, and comes to stand before Sophia.

SOPHIA: Out of the eater came something to eat, and out of the strong came something sweet.

MELISSA: What is sweeter than honey? And what is stronger than a lion?[4]

Sophia lights the candles on the altar; first the blue, then the red. After she lights the black, Melissa takes her place in Binah. After she has lit the white, Sophia takes her place in Chokmah.

SOPHIA: A new star is born, yet the other is not diminished; a

---

4 Judges 14. This is a vastly superior illustration of the formula of Our Lady and the Beast whereon She Rideth than that found in Atu XI, which simplified the formula ad absurdum.

new flame alight in the Holy of Holies, and her Sisters burn ever stronger.

Why am I jealous? Why do you presume? Why do we fear? We have been taught untruth since the cradle. We stand equal—force shared between us is not diminished, but burns brighter and more furiously within the tension of the circuit.

IV
Of the Ceremony of the Opening of the Veil

SOPHIA: Thus, standing strong together as Sisters, we call down the powers.

SOPHIA & MELISSA: [*in unison, with hands outstretched in the Sign of Isis in Welcome[5]*] In the name of our Father Chaos, and our Son Baphomet, and our Spirit, the Fire Qadosh.

MELISSA: I emerged from the great womb already pregnant. With your love that shaketh death, the sweet scent of your whoredom like a seven-stringed instrument, the shaking begins; this shaking which I know will give the peace of satiate lust when He comes.[6]

SOPHIA: O azure-lidded woman, bend upon them![7]
Melissa descends; with the Sign of the Rending of the Veil[8] and a great cry of AHA![9] she wrenches forth Neophutos. She leads him

---

5 See *Liber O, The Signs of the Grades.*
6 The Cry of the 2nd Aethyr, that is called ARN.
7 *Liber AL vel Legis.*
8 See *Liber O, The Signs of the Grades.*
9 AHA = Aleph - Heh - Aleph = 7. It is therefore a God-name of Venus. Interpreted by Yetziratic attribution, it is "The Crossing of our Lady (Heh = the Supernal Mother) in the Air (Aleph)."

to Yesod, where she washes his feet. Thence, she brings him to Tiphareth and stands before him, holding an arrow against his chest.[10]

MELISSA: There is a Swan whose name is Ecstasy: it wingeth from the Deserts of the North; it wingeth through the blue; it wingeth over the fields of rice; at its coming they push forth the green. In all the Universe this Swan alone is motionless; it seems to move, as the Sun seems to move; such is the weakness of our sight. O fool! criest thou? Amen. Motion is relative: there is Nothing that is still. Against this Swan you shot an arrow; the white breast poured forth blood. Men smote you; then, perceiving that you were Nemo, they let you pass. Thus and not otherwise you came to the Temple of the Graal.[11]

*Melissa removes the arrow and returns to Binah.
Neophutos kneels at Da'ath; all congregants kneel[12]*

MELISSA: Despair! Despair! For thou mayest deceive the Virgin, and thou mayest cajole the Mother; but what wilt thou say unto the ancient Whore that is throned in Eternity? For if she will not, there is neither force nor cunning, nor any wit, that may prevail upon her.

Thou canst not woo her with love, for she *is* love. And she hath all, and hath no need of thee.

And thou canst not woo her with gold, for all the Kings and captains of the earth, and all the gods of heaven, have showered

---

10 The Formula of the Dying God is reluctant to expire.
11 The Book of Lies, Chapter 17.
12 All present must kneel, unless physically unable. To refuse to kneel is to claim the temporary body sovereign, which is nothing more than the reification of ego. We are divine; we kneel in awe.

their gold upon her. Thus hath she all, and hath no need of thee.

And thou canst not woo her with knowledge, for knowledge is the thing that she hath spurned. She hath it all, and hath no need of thee.

And thou canst not woo her with wit, for her Lord is Wit.

She hath it all, and hath no need of thee. Despair! Despair!

Nor canst thou cling to her knees and ask for pity; nor canst thou cling to her heart and ask for love; nor canst thou put thine arms about her neck, and ask for understanding; for thou had all these, and they avail thee not. Despair! Despair![13]

NEOPHUTOS:
[softly, with mourning]
A ka dua
Tuf ur biu
Bi a'a chefu
Dudu nur af an nuteru.

Neophutos stands.

[a little louder, with acceptance]
A ka dua
Tuf ur biu
Bi a'a chefu
Dudu nur af an nuteru.

Neophutos comes to stand before the Altar.

[triumphant]
A ka dua
Tuf ur biu

---

13   The Cry of the 2nd Aethyr, that is called ARN

Bi a'a chefu
Dudu nur af an nuteru.

Melissa places her Neophutos upon the altar, and places her veil over him. She stands once more in Binah, with her left hand on Neophutos' left thigh. Neophutos places his finger on his lips, in the Sign of Silence.[14]

SOPHIA: Here remaineth only the Lord of the Aeon, the Avenger, the Child both Crowned and Conquering, the Lord of the Sword and the Sun, the Babe in the Lotus, pure from his birth, the Child of Suffering, the Father of Justice, unto whom be the glory throughout all the Aeon.[15]

V
Of the Office of the Collects

SOPHIA: Lady of Sorrow, that art the might of woman, that art the essence of every Mystery upon the surface of the Earth, continuing knowledge from generation unto generation, thou adored of us upon rivers and seas, within valleys and caves, secretly in our sleeping chambers and openly in our hearts, in temples of tears and flesh and bone as in these other temples of stone, we worthily commemorate them worthy that did of old adore thee and manifest thy glory unto women.

At each name Sophia, with her hand loosely cupped, marks a circle.

Mary Magdalene, Aisha, Helen of Troy, Cleopatra, Hypatia of Alexandria, Sappho, Salome, Bathsheba, Helen of Tyre, Empress

---

14 The Sign of Harpocrates: see Liber O, The Signs of the Grades.
15 The Cry of the 2nd Aethyr, which is called ARN.

Theodora of Byzantium, Sei Shonagon, Morgan Le Fey, Vivian of the Lake, Gwenhwyfar, Esclarmonde de Foix, Lucrezia Borgia, Hildegard von Bingen, Queen Elizabeth I, Catherine of Siena, Simone de Beauvoir, Mary Wollstonecraft, Mary Shelley, Berthe de Corriere, Colette, Ida Craddock, Marie Laveau, Helena Petrovna Blavatsky, Anna Kingsford, Moina Mathers, Rose Kelley, Leila Waddell, Mary D'Este Sturges, Leah Hirsig, Dion Fortune, Ithell Colquhoun, Pamela Colman-Smith, Frieda Lady Harris, Anais Nin, Marjorie Cameron, Phyllis Seckler, Helen Parsons-Smith, Nema Andahadna.

In addition, we commemorate all those ancient priestesses, prophetesses and pythiae whose holiness has been defamed.
Every woman burnt in the witch-trials.
Every mother. Every whore. Every crone.
Every woman that was and is and is to come.
In Our name BABALON
DEDIT![16]

MELISSA: And now appears before my eyes great black Rose, each of whose petals, though it be featureless, is yet a devil-face. And all the stalks are the black snakes of hell. It is alive, this Rose; a single thought informs it. It comes to clutch, to murder. Yet, because a single thought alone informs it, I have hope therein.

I think the Rose has a hundred and fifty-six petals, and though it be black, it has the luminous blush.

Holy, Holy, Holy art thou!
Light, Life and Love are like three glow-worms at thy feet: the

---

16 Dedit = "She gave". It is a secret quality of Our Lady. See DEDIT! in The Drug and Other Stories.

whole universe of stars, the dewdrops on the grass whereon thou walkest!

MELISSA: Before thee all the most holy is profane, O thou desolator of shrines! O thou falsifier of the oracles of truth! Ever as I went, hath it been thus. Again and again the fortress must be battered down! pylon must be overthrown! Again and again must the gods be desecrated!

MELISSA: Aha! Aha!
Yea! Let me take the form of Hadit before theə!

Melissa kneels in adoration, her arms raised above her head; congregation kneels. In adoration, Melissa sings

A ka dua
Tuf ur biu
Bi a'a chefu
Dudu nur af an nuteru.
Nuit! Nuit! Nuit! How art thou manifested in this place! This is a
    Mystery ineffable. And it is mine, and I can never reveal it
either to God or to man. It is for thee and me![17]

VI
Of the Consecration of the Elements (Pentecost)

MELISSA: [*stands in the sign of Isis Rejoicing[18]; congregation stands*]:

---

17 The Cry of the 2nd Aethyr, that is called ARN
18 See Liber O, The Signs of the Grades.

O azure-lidded woman, bend upon them!
Hear the sound like the rushing of a violent wind as it fills the
temple.
See these many tongues of fire rest, one upon each head.
And we are all filled with the Pneumatos Hagiou.
And we all begin to speak.[19]

MELISSA and THE CONGREGANTS: Omari tessala marax,
tessala dodi phornepax.
amri radara poliax
armana piliu.
amri radara piliu son';
mari narya barbiton
madara anaphax sarpedon
andala hriliu. [x3]

*During the chant, Sophia descends to the womb via the Path of
Lightning, pulls forth the bag of wine[20] and brings it to the Altar,
ascending via the Path of the Serpent. Once Sophia has completed
her journey, the congregation may sit.*

SOPHIA: The shedding of blood is necessary, for God did not
hear the Children of Eve until blood was shed.[21]
Blood is shed in Death; but is not blood also shed in the bringing
of Life?
Does not blood flow with the pull of the Moon, as does blood dry

---

19   Book of Acts 2
20   The bag of wine will ideally be made of the bladder of an animal, or of animal skin.
Inside there is wine sweetened with honey, and thickened with a crushed Cake of Light.
This cake should be prepared according to the instructions given in *Liber AL,* with one
difference; in civilised countries, where the option is available, the blood to be used is that
of the placenta and afterbirth flow. If this is not available, menstrual blood will suffice.
21   The Cry of the 2nd Aethyr, which is called ARN

in the heat of the Sun?

Sophia holds the bag of wine aloft toward Kether.

SOPHIA: the blood of the Mother; the blood of the Son.

Sophia hands the bag of wine to Melissa, who holds the bag aloft.

MELISSA: the life in the water; the two that are one.
Is this not the blood of my blood from whence springs life?
Is this not the quickening of all things?
Is this not the beginning and the end?

MELISSA *[Pouring wine over the head of Neophutos]*:
In the name of Our Lady and Our Lord do I anoint thee.
In the name of their Daughter and their Son do I anoint thee.
In the name of the three-in-one and the one-in-three, do I anoint
thee.

Melissa holds the bag aloft.

This is the Aeon of the Immortal Blood.

Melissa places the bag upon the altar.

VII

Of the Office of the Anthem

The congregation stand.

MELISSA *[arms raised and head thrown back]*:
Thou who art I, my secret flame

Who has these natures and these names,
Who art, when these still have not come,
Thou secret centre of the Sun
Thou hidden spring of all things known
And unknown, thou aloof, alone,
Thou, the true blood in the rood
Thou source and seed, thy breed and brood
Thou, Mother of all dark and light
Thou beyond speech and beyond sight,
Thee I invoke, my Bitter Sea
Rising roaring making free.
Thee I invoke, continuous one,
Thee, secret centre of the sun.
And that most holy mystery
Of which the vehicle are we
Appear in fire, appear in rain
For honey rises from the slain.

SOPHIA *[arms raised and head thrown back]:*
For of the Mother and the Child
The Fire Qadosh is both partaken
Tiresias, uncategorised, wild;
In man the woman does awaken.
Glory and worship in the highest
Thou shard that mankind deifiest
Being that race, that learned and lied
And still we find we are not forsaken.
Glory and worship be to thee

Our Mother of the Bitter Sea.

The congregation raise their arms in praise.

SOPHIA, and all on the right: Glory to Thee from chariot patient.

MELISSA, and all on the left: Glory to Thee from chalice ancient.

SOPHIA et al: Glory to Thee from chattel owned.

MELISSA et al: Glory to Thee from queen enthroned.

SOPHIA et al: Glory to Thee, thou regents bold Pogenitors of black and gold.

MELISSA et al: Glory to Thee, thee that I am
Thou lion and thou ailing lamb.

SOPHIA et al: Glory to Thee, thy way we pave
We sing in the nave and we sing in thy cave.

MELISSA et al: Glory to Thee, true Unity
Thou three in one, thou one in three.

ALL: Glory and worship unto Thee,
Our Mother of the Bitter Sea.

VIII

Of the Consummation of the Elements (Fear and Trembling)

SOPHIA [in the Sign of Fire][22]:

---

22   See Liber O, The Signs of the Grades.

To the God OAI
Be praise
In the end and the beginning!

MELISSA [in the Sign of Water][23]: And that which thou hearest is but the dropping of the dew from my limbs, for I dance in the night, naked upon the grass, in shadowy places, by running streams. Many are they who have loved the nymphs of the woods, and of the wells, and of the fountains, and of the hills. And of these some were nympholept. For it was not a nymph, but I myself that walked upon the earth taking my pleasure. So also there were many images of Pan, and men adored them, and as a beautiful god he made their olives bear double and their vines increase; but some were slain by the god, for it was I that had woven the garlands about him.

Every man that hath seen me forgetteth me never, and I appear oftentimes in the coals of the fire, and upon the smooth white skin of woman, and in the constancy of the waterfall, and in the emptiness of deserts and marshes, and upon great cliffs that look seaward; and in many strange places, where men seek me not. And many thousand times he beholdeth me not. And at last I smite myself into him as a vision smiteth into a stone, and whom I call must follow.[24]

Those Congregants who intend to communicate will advance one by one to the Altar.

Each Congregant kneels before Melissa, who pours wine from the bag into their mouth. They rise, and stand before Sophia, who traces the Rose-Cross on their breast with Holy Oil.[25]

---

23   See Liber O, The Signs of the Grades.
24   The Cry of the 2nd Aethyr, which is called ARN
25   Oil of Abramelin is traditional, though not fundamental.

After the Celebration has finished, Sophia, with her hand loosely cupped, marks a circle over the congregants thrice thus:

SOPHIA:
Our Lady bless you.
[traces circle over congregants]

Our Lady enlighten your minds and comfort your hearts and sustain your bodies. [traces circle over congregants]

Our Lady bring you to the accomplishment of your True Will, the Great Work; for this is Her Will, and we are all Her children. [traces circle over congregants]

As the officers were already present in the Temple when the Congregation arrived, so too they remain enthroned as the newly revived Congregation pour forth into the world.

—FINIS—

The Equinox of the Bees
A Contemplation for Persephone's Rising

*"Let my idle chatter be the muttering of prayer, my every manual
movement the execution of ritual gesture, my walking a ceremonial
circumambulation, my eating and other acts the rite of sacrifice,
my lying down, prostration in worship, my every pleasure enjoyed
with dedication of myself, let whatever activity of mine be some
form of worship of you."*

Saundaryalahari, 27

Introduction

There is a great controversy that plagues examinations of body
and spirit. It seems every source tells us we must either be an ascetic,
or a hedonist. Rejecting both, we tread a sad and grim middle path.
Yet there is another way — the both/and. It is possible to be both an
ascetic, and a hedonist. To experience the goddess in every dealing
of the self with the world around us. And this is not a metaphor for
life experiences or astral journeys but a command that every single
movement, every thought, every breath, every bite and stomach
full, that each of these be recognised for its potential to experience
divinity — and for divinity to experience us. The body and spirit
are not distinct. Our gods do not float somewhere above our heads,
nor do they live in trees or temples. They exist in the inbetween —
in the senses, in experience, in the huge multifaceted mass that is

the individual constellation's everflowing experience of life. This contemplation seeks to remind us of the everywhere-ness of the godhead. Of the god in the sense, and the god in the heart — that we are god, that god is us — that we create images, but these are not Her. And yet, they are Her — for every bit of Her can be found in the simple act of pouring a cup of tea.

We seek the byways of the gods. We need gods, though we may make of our gods what we will. There is an infinity of joy to be gained in the regular practice of contemplation and ritual, whatever its form or aim. Of course all this is human, infinitely human, for we humans are infinite constellations. So too none of this is of us, for we are all electricity, with the consciousness of planets.

Preparing the Body

Your personal form of commitment to the Work will dictate the level of preparation you undertake. A period of fasting is always to be recommended before magical work. Three days without meat and dairy is best, followed by the 12 hours leading up to the ritual to be devoid of any food or water. However, in contemporary times we have lost the valuable mechanic of the fast. Thus, the very minimum should be that no food or drink is consumed in the 30 minutes leading up to any ritual work. Physical cleansing is also to be recommended. A bath with tea tree or hyssop followed by anointing with sandalwood or abramelin oil is particularly effective. Simply a hot shower and a change of clothes will also have a potent effect. The bare minimum is a thorough washing of the hands and face. After cleansing, wear what you Will; but whether in yoga pants, robed, or skyclad, be sure that you feel clean and comfortable.

Preparing the Altar

Ingredients:

- Altar
- Tablecloth
- Icon
- Bowl of water
- Teapot and cup
- Flowers or herbs
- Incense and candle
- Paper and pen
- Bloodletting tool, or other offering.
- Food/drink for a feast.

Before you should be an altar; a small table, or even a space cleared on the floor, covered with a tablecloth or scarf. A circular altar the ideal for this work, but is not necessary. Upon the altar should be: an image that, to you, signifies Our Lady. Perhaps a septagram, or Our Lady in whichever of Her faces patronises you; or a bee. Between that icon and you should lie a bowl of water.[1] There must also be, either upon the altar or close to it, the preparations for tea.[2] This may be done according to your will, but there must be a teapot, filled, and a tea cup, empty. Ideally these should be the best you have, or precious in some other sense. The tea should ideally be

---

1 Water from natural springs is always the best for magical work; second is water from the river or the sea, third is water collected from the rain. If circumstances dictate you must use water from the tap, it must be purified with salt.
2 The bowl of water and the cup of tea represent the two altar-pools found at the temple of Demeter and Persephone at Akragas.

of something bitter, such as green tea with tumeric, or tea made from mugwort or other bitter herbs. Salty tea, prepared according to the mongolian or indian styles, is also ideal. There should be flowers. Cuttings from one's own land or garden is always ideal, but a bunch of fresh flowers is equally good. Dried or plastic are also acceptable, so too are bunches of fragrant herbs. A bunch of basil or thyme is readily available, inexpensive and easy to grow (even as a pot plant), and will serve well as visual and olfactory stimulus. Upon the altar should be incense burning,[3] and a candle lit.

Moving into Stillness

With your body and altar thus prepared, it is time to come to the temple. Take some time to stretch out your body, moving into the physicality and sensation. Find a comfortable position seated before the altar. Hero pose is ideal, if you are able to hold it for an hour without ache. Cross legged is also very good. A cushion or chair is also okay — it is important that you are able to sit comfortably. However, whichever position you take, it is important that you maintain the proper posture. Sit on the front edge of your sitting bones, with a slight arch in your lower back. Do not lean back, but sit upright, as though your head is being raised on an invisible string. With the sit bones forward and the midriff erect, pull the shoulders up and back, becoming even more erect without thrusting the chest out. Lift your head from the middle, not the front, and tuck your chin slightly.

Try to maintain this posture throughout. You should not be strained or uncomfortable — if you do not have a regular practice

---

3   Sweet incense are to be preferred, such as those fragranced with flowers and honey, or green frankincense. Otherwise, abramelin incense is always acceptable for work with Our Lady.

of sitting, this may be difficult, so go easy on yourself. No not allow yourself to slump, but equally do not strain — try to find ease and a sense of flight as you sit. But this should feel like exercise, and work — the proper mode of sitting is in itself an example of movement-in-stillness, of dynamic passivity.

Now, come to regulate your breath. Take a look inside your mind, as you did your body. Do not strain for emptiness, but come to a sense of equilibrium, of energy in stillness. Do not carve out space for this work, but contemplate where the space already exists.

As with the mental, so with the physical: provided you are in a comfortable temple space, no banishing or circle-drawing is required for this rite. If these things help you to compose yourself for the Work, then so be it: but Our Mother is everywhere and all, and any spatial delineation or attempt to divide between good and bad aspects of the spirits of things is arbitrary. Instead of attempting to delineate sacred space and mundane space, aim to intensify the presence of She who is the Glory of the World.

Performing the Rite

This rite may be performed in one of two ways, depending on the constitution of the one who would perform it. It may be performed with a partner, through reading aloud the passages marked Spoken below. This option requires the most concentration, and offers the most margin for lapse. It may be performed with a partner, where the partner, sitting on the opposite side of the bowl, reads aloud. I would only caution that this should be performed with a magical partner, and one should expect the consequences of partnered work with Our Lady.

Through the following sections, whether you are speaking or

listening, you should visualise all that is said as vividly as possible, imbuing it with emotional vigor. However if you find your sense wandering, two things may be used to assist you.

First, throughout the duration of this rite, maintain the integrity of your posture. As you visualise do not ignore the body — this is not astral travel, but a journey inside. If your mind wanders return it to the inside work via the body — check in with how you feel, how your seat is, if any adjustment is needed, etc.

Second, if the use of a tattwa would be useful for your work, a downward-pointing triangle of red is most appropriate, and may be visualised any time you feel the focus of your contemplation wander.

I. The Blessing of the Bee

As the blessing is recited, one should clasp the hands and touch the crown of the head, the heart, the two shoulders, and the lips, before throwing the hands up and out for the final two lines.

Spoken:

Honour to the mother, and to the mother's mother. Honour to all
my teachers, and all those who have gone before.

The golden dust of pollen for my crown
The dance of devotion in my heart
The powers of flight spread from my shoulders
The sweetness of honey upon my lips.
Io Demeter, Bitter Sea
Io honeyed one, Persephone

II.Gloria Mundi
(The Adoration of the Senses)

A key aim of this practice (which can be performed every day, or every week) is the cultivation the sense-capacities, and the divinity of the sensory processes. We thus aim to reconcile our arbitrary separation of the sacred and the mundane, and so learn to find god in every mundane movement — and to find mundanity even in the spiritual depths. Through regular work of this kind one may learn to make of the whole world a Temple; and this is one path to the Priesthood of She.

All should be done deliberately, with intention. Not stiffly, but seeing the body as a vehicle of Will, and the nexus of the experiences of pleasure and joy. Try to take pleasure and joy in this simple act of pouring tea. With each section the first sentence should be spoken, then the ritualist should perform the appropriate action, then the remaining line or lines should be spoken.

Spoken:

I pick up the tea pot. I feel the porcelain beneath my fingers, the weight within my hand. In this fired and painted earth I feel the body of Our Lady.

I pour the tea. I hear the flow of water from the spout, the answering echo of the cup. In the song of the water, I hear the laughter of Our Lady as She takes pleasure in Her caves.

I settle my gaze onto the cup. I see the lights playing on the surface of the water. I see the steam rise in coils towards the sky. As my eyes follow these movements I glimpse the fleeting form of Our Lady as She dances.

I close my eyes and, raising the cup, I inhale its scent. I breathe in the perfume of Our Lady's waters, the perspiration of Her skin.

I take a sip. As the hot liquid fills my mouth I taste Her. She is the honeyed one; yet Her waters are Bitter like the Sea.

I swallow Her, and feel Her fill my belly, Her heat rising to my heart. I see her residing there. Clothed in space, of a hue as red as dawn, drenched in the nectar of ecstasy.

She stands amidst a sacred pool. I contemplate Our Lady upon the water; the goddess dancing in my heart.

III. Exploration of the Inside

Spoken, and visualised:

And as the goddess dances and sings in my heart I feel the lines of fire and water that radiate this centre.

I feel the flow of blood and of bile, the tides and waves. I contemplate how my body feels, and how I feel about it. I locate areas of discomfort, or pleasure. I have experienced the sweetness and bitterness of my senses; now I taste the honey and salt inside of me. I do not judge nor discriminate, only feel. I bring awareness to the inside of my skin, to my muscles, and my blood.

I explore the rivers and caves of my body as if it is some dark unknown continent. I consider the meeting places and the shrines, the fields and the caves. I explore the sea, and follow the channels up to their source.

I contemplate the cave paintings on the inside of my skull. I remember my mind is part of my body, too. I consider the places of discomfort and of pleasure there, the honey and the salt, the markets and shrines. Once more I do not judge, reject, dissociate or revel. I only feel; the sensations, the half-formed thoughts, desires. I am

aware. I consider their source. I seek the centre.

I contemplate my journeying. I undertake a pilgrimage to the darkest caves. In the depths, there is the heavy drone of bees; this is the nursery of the nymphs. Before the carven altar of this honeyed temple there waits a silent, dark pool. The surface of the pool is perfect, like glass or a mirror. Yet it flows; deep in the earth the silent spring bubbles. The pool appears still but is ever-moving, ever-new. I feel this dark pool within me. Feel the silent currents and ancient springs bubble through my blood. I feel my body, watery yet solid. Strong in its passivity; supine yet ever-ready.

In my contemplation, I come to stillness. Still, but not stiff. I feel my body strong in its passiveness, relaxed yet ready. I bring my awareness to the constant vibrations that echo through my body, the low drone of the bees who guard the sacred pool. I listen to the song of my cells, the low hum. I am aware that, even in stillness, I possess an infinite potential for movement and growth. My very materiality is a storehouse of energy; and this stillness I inhabit is as energetic a choice as an ecstatic dance. I dance in the stillness.

I bring my awareness to the pillar of light that ascends my spine. I explore it; I touch it gently with my mind, feel the sparks and flow. I look closely, and see that it is not one line, but two, an ever-twisting double-helix of light, dancing and playing eternally through the pathways of my body. This is the source of life and of death. I contain within me the creation of the universe, and the destruction of eternity. All this — and yet these forces are perfectly balanced within this delicate sphere called I.

IV. Composition of the Garden Temple

Spoken, and visualised:

Now I imagine this vibrating stillness called I finds itself in a garden. I fill my senses with the place. I feel the warmth of the earth beneath me, the tickle of the beetle crawling over my foot, the soft breeze playing over my bare skin. The scent of grass, and steaming earth, and flowers and wild herbs. The lazy lolling drone of bees, and the song of birds overhead.

I open my eyes to the garden. It is more beautiful and more perfect than any earthly garden, here in the valley in the high mountains, where the purple phoenix makes its nest. The grass in the garden is long and lush, and scattered all about are patches of wild wheat and corn. With the bursting Spring of contemplation my flowers bloom. To the south is a thick swathe of poppies, spilling bloody droplets over the red clay. To the north, a heavy stand of lilies, their whiteness defying the dark earth. To the west there is a grove of pomegranate trees, thick with fruit and flower. Dittany grows around the outcrops of the valley's walls.

All this is so much exquisite background, for I am seated facing east, by a pool wherein all this beautiful garden is reflected, quivering. Seated at the edge of the pool, I am reflected too. Yet the reflection is something more than me — it shines and vibrates, and jerks and moves and spirals with the current, seen out the corner of my eye. At the far side of the pool, its roots and weeping branches breaking the water, stands a willow, its ancient branches twisted with ivy. The trunk of the willow is hollow, and therein a drift of bees has made their nest. The whole tree hums, and drips with honey. At the foot of the tree grows a plant with shining black berries. It is the fruit of Our Lady of beauty and death. And the hollow trunk of the tree

is the form of a woman; the most perfect figure of art it is possible to contemplate, flowing and flawed with the knots of the wood and dripping, ever dripping, with honey.

She dances on the water, too — in the watery pool the goddess and I dance and sing in the garden. Yet, all is still and quiet, but for the busy drone of the bees.

In the distance, I hear a gentle wail, as of a mother searching for her child. In the distance, a voice comes in answer — "Mother, I am coming. Mother, I am coming home."

And as the garden spills its sparkling life before me, and the plants and the insects dance and love and pray, I cast my offering into the pool. It is a little tangle of pale pink dust, tied up in an old white handkerchief. I cast this piteous gift into the water, This piteous gift which is everything I am, everything I have, everything I might ever be.

And I say: I am noone.

And the dust in the kerchief mixes with the water, and it's rising falling dance like smoke betrays the secret currents therein. For this pool is fed by the same springs that feed that other pool. For this is Her land. The Garden is the crown of Her caves.

V. Invocation of Our Lady Rising

In the darkness there is single head of wheat.
With a scythe the head is cut.

Still in the seated position, assume the arms of Isis in Welcome.

Spoken:

I appear like the early morning rays of the Sun.
My teeth are perfect, pearly black, black bees between red lips

perfectly curved across the circle of my face, rising like the dawn. A curved half moon upon my forehead, my eyes impenetrable in my reddened brow.

My arms like the crescent of the moon, only more perfect.

My lithe, playful hands with their glinting nails are wrapped around a simple golden Cup of exquisite craftsmanship.

My rising breasts lie gleaming, pendulous upon the starry expanse of my chest.

Upon my beautiful, mountainous belly is the Monuments of Nations. My round hips lie like precious jewels, or mountains amidst the sea. I wear a girdle of starry rubies.

I am veiled all in red silk, a gauze transparent in its fineness. I am adorned with red gems, set in gold.

My redness is the redness of the rose, or of red earth, or of pomegranate seeds.

My beautiful body, lithe as a gazelle but for the perfect protrusion of my belly.

My whole body hums, like the drone of the honeybee. In my Form is infinite Force.

Smeared with red earth, I am the vanquisher of the God of Love. I stand in a pool of the sweetest water, for immortality flows from my vulva.

The Great Beast lies down to drink from my pool.

I am the Sacred Courtesan. The Harlot that Shaketh Death. I am the Blasphemed Against, the Beaten and Broken, the Rising Up.

I am the Mother of Life and the Birth of Destruction. Mine is the most Holy and Sacred Cup of Fornications.

VI. The Sacrifice

Dwell with the knowledge of yourself in godform. Open your eyes, and breathe this image in its vitality into the icon in front of you. Seven times breathe the living image of the goddess into the icon. Focus your gaze upon the icon, see Our Lady inhabit it, see Her one with it, as She inhabits and is one with you.

It is now time to offer a sacrifice to Our Lady. First, make sure a candle and incense are lit upon the altar. Then, make your offering. Ideally this will be a promise, a dedication, an intention; a concrete act in the future, or a dedication to Her every month, or every moment. This should be written on a slip of paper, anointed with blood, and burnt, with the ashes scattered into the bowl of water. Alternatively, this may be spoken aloud as blood or ink is dropped into the water.

If such an offering does not appeal (or in addition, if that be your will), flowers or fruit or sweet things may be offered. Remember quality is always to be prioritised before quantity. Our Lady is Lady of the Earth, which is Dying. A single square of fine chocolate, a spray of rosemary, or an apple are preferable to a jumbo box of chocolates, fifty roses, or a basket of exotic fruit.

Our Lady is Lady of Song, so it is particularly fitting to cement

your promise with a mantra or song. One in particular is most suitable and holy for work with Our Lady:

Spoken or sung:

Omari tessala marax,
tessala dodi phornepax.
amri radara poliax
armana piliu.
amri radara piliu son';
mari narya barbiton
madara anaphax sarpedon
andala hriliu.[4]

VII. Contemplation

It is now time to compose oneself to receive Her blessing. Once more find stillness. Feel the energy in this stillness, and understand that receptiveness is not a passive act, but an active one. Take the image of the goddess before you and once more breathe it seven times into your heart. Do not yearn for the Goddess, but dwell with Her. Feel Her ever-present flame. Fill every sense with Her, as earlier you found Her in the arrows of every sense. She is that to which every experience must be offered. Inflame yourself in prayer.

You should now undertake a period of contemplation. How long you spend depends entirely on how long you, personally, can maintain concentration. This might be anything from ten seconds to an hour. In order to ease concentration, you may wish to to use a mantra to aid your meditation here. It is best if this is something that

4 From *The Cry of the 2nd Aethyr,* which is called ARN.

is easily memorizable and repeatable. The mantra "Ave Babalon," sung seven times, is ideal. Alternatively you may use Omari tessala marax once again. You may also choose to use the first lines of the Homeric Hymn to Demeter, which would be particularly effective here, and are as follows:

Demeter nukomon,
semnen theon,
arcom aeidein,
auten ede thugatra tanusphoron

Δήμητρ' ἠύκομον,
σεμνὴν θεόν,
ἄρχομ' ἀείδειν,
αὐτὴν ἠδὲ θύγατρα τανύσφυρον

I sing of Demeter,
the holy goddess with the golden hair,
and of Her daughter, too

You are equally welcome to use a mantra personal to your own Work with Her, or one relevant to your chosen form of the goddess.

The Feast

Work with Our Lady should always be followed by a feast. This is a mark of respect, and the logical outcome of a sacrificial act. It is also a practical matter; eating and drinking brings the forces back to earth. This is a lone rite, and so here the usual communal feast takes new forms. One may choose to share a meal or a bowl of fruit with Our Lady, dedicating to Her every aspect of the experience;

finding Her in the joy of taste and texture (as in the tea ceremony above). The experience of pleasure is dedicated to Her — and in the same movement, that experience of pleasure is the experience of Her. The feast may be naught more than a cup of hot tea or coffee, with every sip taken a microcosm of the movement of Her Great Bitter Seas; yet the meal should be well considered: it is better to have warm water with a slice of lemon from a favourite cup, than a chain-restaurant pizza in a cardboard tray. The intake of earthly nourishment should be accompanied with a sense of connection to Her; in time one should learn to find Her in every such act — but for now, in thanks for what She has given on this day, this feast will be unto Her.

Epilogue

There is a sweetness to Her presence. Bombarded as we are with sugar, and all things light and nice, we forget that good honey is so sweet it is almost painful on the tongue.

One may spend one hour every day in mediation and Work; but if this time is sectioned off from so-called normal life, then this is wasted. One's relationship with the divine is the Work, but it is not work as we have grown to know it. To meditate according to the clock, 30 mins every morning — this is the ultimate itemization of the spiritual path. Thus the box can be ticked, the spiritual has been achieved rather than experienced.

What is sex magic? It is learning to understand the divinity of sex, and the divinity available through sex. It is not black candles and a circle on the floor. We magicians rejected the gods and ended up with a tradition of lip-service. There are no part-time adepts. So too with food — is it any wonder we cannot inhabit our bodies, cannot

remember every consumption is an intaking of the goddess, when the food-systems of which we are a part are so utterly monstrous? But that is not a reason not to try — to understand every single piece of food and drink one puts in one's body, just as much as every dealing with the man on the street, or every prayer and creation, is a dealing with Our Lady, a face-to-face with the divine.

The principles of right eating are simple, yet they cannot be tricked or traded. We have commodified and commercialised our world until it is easy, the easiest thing, to live a life devoid of joy. In this climate, the greatest resistance is joy. Pure, unbridled, unbounded, joy. Understand that joy is found in the interstices of the body with the outside world, and all is transformed. Now eat those ground-up, antibiotic-filled chicken feet and tell me, do you feel joy? Now try this kheer, brown rice cooked slow in milk, with fruit and spices. Is this not the sustenance of Our Lady's breast? Eat in a way that soothes and fuels your body. Eat according to the season, your locale, and your means. And eat for joy. Switch off the tv, put down the book, and consider what you do as you eat. Find the experience of Our Lady there.

www.ingramcontent.com/pod-product-compliance
Lightning Source LLC
Chambersburg PA
CBHW030854090426
42737CB00009B/1222